Extra Support Copying Masters

Grade 1

 Harcourt School Publishers

www.harcourtschool.com

Printed in the United States of America

ISBN 10: 0-15-349866-8
ISBN 13: 978-0-15-349866-4

6 7 8 9 10   862   17 16 15 14 13 12 11 10 09 08

Contents

SPRING FORWARD—BOOK 1–1

Lesson 1 Let's Tap! 2–7
Lesson 2 The Van 9–14
Lesson 3 Big Rigs 16–21
Lesson 4 Get Up, Rick! 23–28
Lesson 5 Dot and Bob 30–35
Lesson 6 All on the Map 37–42

ZOOM ALONG—BOOK 1–2

Lesson 7 Little Red Hen Gets Help 2–7
Lesson 8 Beth's Job 9–14
Lesson 9 Plants Can't Jump 16–21
Lesson 10 Soccer Song 23–28
Lesson 11 Land of Ice 30–35
Lesson 12 King Midas and His Gold 37–42

REACH FOR THE STARS—BOOK 1–3

Lesson 13 A Butterfly Grows 2–7
Lesson 14 Mark's Big Day 9–14
Lesson 15 Tomás Rivera 16–21
Lesson 16 One More Friend 23–28
Lesson 17 Can Elephants Paint? 30–35
Lesson 18 Snow Surprise 37–42

MAKE YOUR MARK—BOOK 1–4

Lesson 19 Little Rabbit's Tale 2–7
Lesson 20 Ways People Live 9–14
Lesson 21 Flake, the Missing Hamster 16–21
Lesson 22 We're Going on a Picnic! 23–28
Lesson 23 On Saturday 30–35
Lesson 24 Mystery of the Night Song 37–42

WATCH THIS!—BOOK 1–5

Lesson 25 Amazing Animals 2–7
Lesson 26 Blast off! 9–14
Lesson 27 Ebb and Flo and the Baby Seal 16–21
Lesson 28 At the Crayon Factory 23–28
Lesson 29 Sand Castle 30–35
Lesson 30 Frog and Toad Together 37–42
Answer Key A1

Extra Support
© Harcourt • Grade 1

Spring Forward

Book 1-1

▶ **Say the picture name. Write <u>a</u> if it has the same middle sound as <u>cat</u>.**

1.

v a n

2.

h ___ t

3.

s ___ n

4.

b ___ g

5.

m ___ p

6.

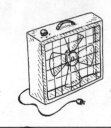

f ___ n

7.

h ___ n

8.

h ___ m

9.

d ___ g

School–Home Connection

Ask your child to say each short *a* word.
Together, think of other short *a* words.

2

Extra Support
© Harcourt • Grade 1 • Book 1

▶ **Look at each picture. Circle the word
that names the picture.**

1.	2.	3.
sag (bag) bat	wag car cap	bat lab sat
4.	5.	6.
map pat nap	lad can cap	fan tan man
7.	8.	9.
mat map yam	wag pan pad	mad tap jam

School–Home Connection
Ask your child to read each word aloud to you.

4

Extra Support
© Harcourt • Grade 1 • Book 1

▶ **Circle the word that best completes each sentence. Write the word.**

help   let's

_____
- - - - - - - - - - - - - - - -

1. I can _____ .

help   now

_____
- - - - - - - - - - - - - - - -

2. We can nap _____ .

Help   Let's

_____
- - - - - - - - - - - - - - - -

3. _____ nap.

School–Home Connection

Have your child read each sentence to you.
Encourage your child to use the words in other
sentences.

5

Extra Support
© Harcourt • Grade 1 • Book 1

▶ **Look at the picture. Read the two words. Write the word in the sentence to tell what will happen. The first one is done for you.**

bat   wag

1. Cat can _____**bat**_____.

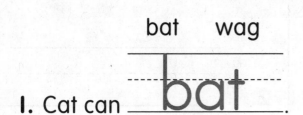

---

sat   ran

2. Cat _____.

---

nap   map

3. Cat has a _____.

School–Home Connection

Have your child read each sentence aloud.
Have your child predict what might happen
next.

Extra Support
© Harcourt • Grade 1 • Book 1

Name _____

▶ **Put together the word and the word ending. Then write the new word.**

hat ⊃⊂ s   map ⊃⊂ s

1. hats   2. _____

bag ⊃⊂ s   van ⊃⊂ s

3. _____   4. _____

wag ⊃⊂ s   tap ⊃⊂ s

5. _____   6. _____

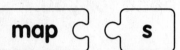

School–Home Connection

Have your child read each completed word
aloud to you. Then ask him or her to say each
completed word in a sentence.

7

Name _____

► **Look at each picture. Circle the word
that names the picture.**

1.

(cat)   cap   fat

2.

pan   van   yam

3.

map   nap   man

4.

has   jam   ham

5.

man   fan   fat

6.

bag   tap   tag

7.

bat   mat   ram

8.

cat   hat   had

9.

rag   tan   ran

School–Home Connection

Ask your child to point to each picture and
say its name. Then have him or her read
each word.

9

▶ **Trace the word. Then read the sentence.**

1. Pam has a ___**map**___.

2. Dan has a ___**cap**___.

3. Max ___**naps**___.

4. Jan can ___**bat**___.

5. The ___**cat**___ ran.

School–Home Connection

Have your child read each sentence aloud.
Point to each picture and talk about how each
sentence tells about the picture.

11

► **Circle the word that best completes each sentence. Write the word.**

in   an

_____

1. My cat sat _____ a bag.

---

too   tan

_____

2. Pat has a cat, _____ .

---

go   no

_____

3. Dan has _____ cat.

School–Home Connection

Read each sentence with your child. Encourage your child to say the words *in, too,* and *no* in other sentences.

Extra Support
© Harcourt • Grade 1 • Book 1

▶ **Look at each picture. Then circle the sentence that tells what will happen next. The first one has been done for you.**

1.

Jan ran out.

(Jan had a nap.)

2.

Max ran a lap.

Max has ham.

3.

The cat ran.

He pats the cat.

School–Home Connection

Have your child describe what is happening in each picture. Then ask him or her what might happen next. Help your child as he or she reads the sentences.

13

Name _____

▶ **Write ag or and to complete each word.**

1. I am in a **band**.

2. Nan has a r_____.

3. Dad has my h_____.

4. I am in the s_____.

5. Max has a b_____.

School–Home Connection
Have your child read each sentence aloud.
Ask which words rhyme with *tag.* (*rag, bag*)
Then ask which words rhyme with *and.* (*band, hand, sand*)

14

Extra Support
© Harcourt • Grade 1 • Book 1

▶ **Say the name of each picture. Write i̱**
if you hear the same middle sound as
in the word wi̱g.

1.

w i g

2.

p _ g

3.

p _ n

4.

d _ g

5.

d _ g

6.

f _ n

7.

h _ ll

8.

m _ k

9.

l _ mp

School–Home Connection

Point to each picture and ask your child to say
its name. Then have him or her copy the short *i*
words on a sheet of paper and draw pictures
for them.

Extra Support

Name _____

▶ **Look at each picture. Circle the word that names the picture.**

1.

(six) sax sit

2.

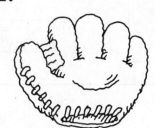

miss mat mitt

3.

pan pin pit

4.

hat his hit

5.

wig wag win

6.

lit lip lap

7.

fist fast fit

8.

list lad lid

9.

did dig dad

School–Home Connection

Have your child put a checkmark by the words that have the short *i* sound in the middle as in *sit*.

18

▶ **Circle the word that best completes the sentence. Write the word.**

1.

Hold　　Get

_____

- - - - - - - - - - - - - - - -

_____ in, Dad!

2.

so　　soon

_____

- - - - - - - - - - - - - - - -

It is _____ fast!

3.

Home　　Hold

_____

- - - - - - - - - - - - - - - -

_____ my hand!

4.

soon　　get

_____

- - - - - - - - - - - - - - - -

It will land _____.

5.

hold　　home

_____

- - - - - - - - - - - - - - - -

Let's go _____, Dad.

School–Home Connection

Together, read each completed sentence aloud.
Point to each circled word and ask your child
to say the word in another sentence.

Extra Support

▶ **Look at the first item in each row.
Circle the two things that are like the
first one. The first one is done for you.**

1.

2.

3.

4.

School–Home Connection

Name two items in your home that are alike.
Have your child tell you how they are the
same. Then ask your child to think of two
things that are the same.

20

Extra Support
© Harcourt • Grade 1 • Book 1

▶ **Draw a line to match the two words with the contraction.**

1. it is   he's

2. here is   she's

3. he is   here's

4. she is   it's

5. where is   what's

6. what is   that's

7. there is   where's

8. that is   there's

School–Home Connection
Read each contraction with your child. Take
turns saying it in a sentence.

21

Extra Support
© Harcourt • Grade 1 • Book 1

▶ **Look at each picture. Circle the word that names the picture.**

1.

tap   tag   (tack)

2.

band   back   bag

3.

lick   lit   lap

4.

sack   sick   six

5.

kid   kiss   kick

6.

sand   sack   sat

School–Home Connection

Help your child read the words aloud. Talk about how the words that name each picture are the same. (They all end with the same sound spelled *ck*.)

23

▶ **Write the word from the box that names each picture.**

| back | kick | lick | sack | sick | tack |

1. _____

2. _____

3. _____

4. _____

5. _____

6. _____

 School–Home Connection

Have your child read each word aloud. Talk about how the words are alike and how they are different.

25

Extra Support
© Harcourt • Grade 1 • Book 1

▶ **Circle the word that best completes the sentence. Write the word.**

late   lit

_____

- - - - - - - - - - - - - - - - - -

1. I am _____.

_____

Oh   Out

_____

- - - - - - - - - - - - - - - - - -

2. _____ no! Will Dad get his gift?

_____

Yam   Yes

_____

- - - - - - - - - - - - - - - - - -

3. _____, he will!

School–Home Connection

Together, read each sentence aloud. Point to the words *oh*, *late*, and *yes* and have your child say each word in a sentence.

26

▶ **Write 1, 2, and 3 to put the pictures in story order. The first one is done for you.**

▶ **Draw a picture about the ending.**

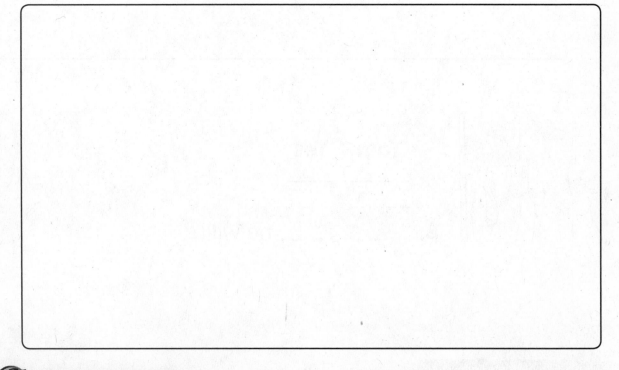

School–Home Connection
Talk about the story in the pictures with your
child. Have your child explain the ending picture.

27

Extra Support
© Harcourt • Grade 1 • Book 1

▶ **Circle the word that best completes each sentence. Write the word.**

(fill) fit

fill

1. I _____ the bag.

---

sill   sit

_____

2. I _____ down.

---

will   wit

_____

3. Jack _____ bat now.

---

ill   it

_____

4. I like _____.

---

hill   hit

_____

5. Let's go up the _____.

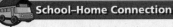 **School–Home Connection**

Have your child read each completed sentence aloud. Talk about how the word choices for each item are alike and how they are different.

28

Name _____

▶ **Name each picture. Write <u>o</u> if you hear the same middle sound as <u>fox</u>.**

1.
_____
- - - - - - -

2.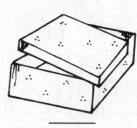
_____
- - - - - - -

3.
_____
- - - - - - -

4.
_____
- - - - - - -

5.
_____
- - - - - - -

6.
_____
- - - - - - -

7.
_____
- - - - - - -

8.
_____
- - - - - - -

School–Home Connection

Find things in the house whose names have the short o sound as in mop.

30

Name _____

▶ **Draw a circle around the name of the picture. Color all the pictures.**

1. 	2. 	3. 
pop (mop) hop	pot sob lot	six box fox
4. 	5. 	6. 
lock log rock	sack sock sit	fog jog log
7. 	8. 	9.
rod rock odd	doll dot dock	bill box bin

🚌 **School–Home Connection**

Have your child read each picture name and point to the letter that stands for the short o sound—the sound in the middle of *mop*.

32

Extra Support
© Harcourt • Grade 1 • Book 1

▶ **Circle the word that best completes each sentence. Write the word.**

thank   much

1. Rick will _____ Bob.

find   much

2. Lil hops too _____.

find   thank

3. I will _____ the mop.

hold   much

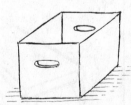

4. There is not _____ in the box.

late   thank

5. I _____ my pal.

School–Home Connection

Read the sentences with your child. Talk about why the word in the blank makes sense in the sentence. Ask your child to say another sentence with the word.

33

▶ **Look at the picture. Read the sentence and the words. Write the word that names the character. The first one is done for you.**

Cat   box

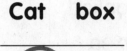

1. Cat sits in a box. ___Cat___

_____

fast   Dog

2. Dog ran fast. _____

_____

Jill   doll

3. Jill has a doll. _____

School–Home Connection

Read aloud the sentences with your child. Talk about the character named in each sentence.

▶ **Read the chart. Then write the word with -ed or -ing that completes each sentence.**

look	+ ing	=	looking
thank	+ ed	=	thanked
mix	+ ed	=	mixed
kick	+ ed	=	kicked
camp	+ ing	=	camping

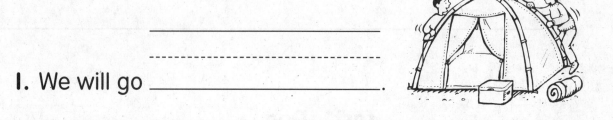

1. We will go _____.

2. Jim _____ Tom for his gift.

3. Rick _____ to me.

4. Dad is _____ for my sock.

 **School–Home Connection**

Have your child read aloud the completed
sentences. Point to the word your child wrote.
Ask what ending was added.

35

▶ **Write the word from the box that names the picture.**

| fall | call | hall | tall | ball | wall |

I.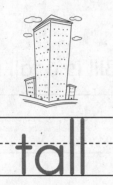

t‍all

2.

_____

3.

_____

4.

_____

5.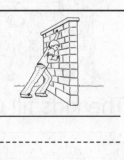

_____

6.

_____

School–Home Connection

Have your child read each word aloud. Talk about how the words are alike and how they are different.

37

▶ **Read the sentences. Circle the words that have the same vowel sound as wall. Write the words on the lines.**

1. Hal will (call) Sam.

call

2. Bill is a tall man.

3. Pam will kick the ball.

4. Jill is at the mall.

5. We all go to the mill.

6. The kids fill up the hall.

School–Home Connection

Help your child read each sentence aloud. Ask him or her to tell you how the circled words are alike.

39

▶ **Circle the word that best completes the sentence. Write the word.**

some   sad
_____
- - - - - - - - - - - - - - - - - - - -
1. I want _____ jam.

make   milk
_____
- - - - - - - - - - - - - - - - - - - -
2. Can you _____ me one?

of   out
_____
- - - - - - - - - - - - - - - - - - - -
3. I want some _____ that.

His   How
_____
- - - - - - - - - - - - - - - - - - - -
4. _____ do you do that?

🚌 **School–Home Connection**

Help your child read each completed sentence
aloud. Say the sentence with the wrong word
and have him or her correct you.

Extra Support
© Harcourt • Grade 1 • Book 1

▶ **Look at the first item in each row. Circle the two things that are like the first one. The first one is done for you.**

1.

2.

3.

4.

 School–Home Connection

Talk about how the pictures are alike and how they are different. Have your child draw a picture of something else that belongs in one of the groups.

41

▶ **Draw a line to match each pair of words with its contraction. The first one has been done for you.**

1. is not ●   ● can't

2. can not ●   ● didn't

3. are not ●   ● aren't

4. did not ●   ● isn't

_____

5. he is ●   ● he's

6. she is ●   ● that's

7. that is ●   ● who's

8. who is ●   ● she's

42

Zoom Along

Book 1-2

▶ **Look at each picture. Circle the word that names the picture.**

1.	2.	3.

bib (bed) red	let pot pet	nest not neck

4.	5.	6.

hen men hop	bib web wet	tell ten tan

7.	8.	9.
		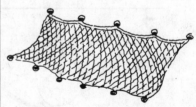
jet get jog	log led leg	not net next

School–Home Connection

Have your child read each word and point to
the letter that makes the short e sound, as
in *bed*.

2

Extra Support
© Harcourt • Grade 1 • Book 2

Name _____

▶ **Say the name of each picture. Write e only if the name has the short e sound, as in bed.**

1.

e g g

2.

m ___ n

3.

b ___ ll

4.

t ___ nt

5.

b ___ ll

6.

l ___ mp

7.

n ___ ck

8.

cl ___ ck

9.

d ___ sk

School–Home Connection

Have your child find things in your home whose names have the short e sound, as in *egg*.

4

Extra Support
© Harcourt • Grade 1 • Book 2

Name _____

▶ **Write the word that best completes the sentence.**

was   hat   as

_____

- - - - - - - - - - - - - - - -

1. The sink _____ a mess.

sad   said   set

_____

- - - - - - - - - - - - - - - -

2. Dad _____ to help.

fit   fix   first

_____

- - - - - - - - - - - - - - - -

3. "I want to nap _____."

eat   end   egg

_____

- - - - - - - - - - - - - - - -

4. "I want to _____."

top   tin   time

_____

- - - - - - - - - - - - - - - -

5. "No, it's _____ to help."

School–Home Connection

Have your child say a sentence, using one of the words he or she wrote, that tells why it is important to be helpful.

5

Extra Support

Name _____

▶ **Look at the pictures. Think about how the animals are the same.**

▶ **Draw a picture in the box to show another animal that is the same.**

 **School–Home Connection**

Have your child describe the animals. Talk about how they are the same and different.

 6

Name _____

▶ **Write bl, cl, fl, or pl to complete
each word.**

1. The land is not _____at.

2. Do you see that _____ock?

3. Hal likes his _____ocks.

4. Hal _____aps his hands.

5. He _____ans to add ten.

School–Home Connection

Have your child blend the letters of each
underlined pair in the directions. Ask your
child to read each sentence aloud.

Extra Support

▶ **Say the name of each picture. Write th
only if the name has the same sound as
at the end of Beth.**

1.

ba

2.

ba

3.
2 + 3 = 5

ma

4.

ca

5.

mi

6.

pa

7.
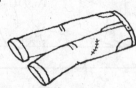

pan

8.

clo

9.

ha

School–Home Connection

Have your child say the name of each picture.
Together, think of other words that begin or
end with the *th* sound, as in *bath*.

9

► **Circle the word that completes each sentence. Then write the word.**

math   thank

_____

- - - - - - - - - - - - - -

1. I do my _____.

bath   with

_____

- - - - - - - - - - - - - -

2. The dog gets a _____.

This   Beth

_____

- - - - - - - - - - - - - -

3. _____ helps me dig.

math   thin

_____

- - - - - - - - - - - - - -

4. The cat is _____.

That   Cloth

_____

- - - - - - - - - - - - - -

5. _____ dog is sick.

School–Home Connection

Ask your child to think of words that have *th* in them. Help him or her make a list.

▶ **Write the word that best completes each sentence.**

says   sets   sells

_____

- - - - - - - - - - - - - - - - - -

1. Nick _____ he will help.

_____

was   water   with

_____

- - - - - - - - - - - - - - - - - -

2. He will _____ the plants.

_____

hen   has   her

_____

- - - - - - - - - - - - - - - - - -

3. Mom likes _____ plants.

_____

dot   don't   dog

_____

- - - - - - - - - - - - - - - - - -

4. I _____ have a mop.

_____

not   net   new

_____

- - - - - - - - - - - - - - - - - -

5. This mop is _____.

School–Home Connection

Have your child read each word and sentence aloud. Together, make up other sentences using the words *line* and *Mr.*

Extra Support
© Harcourt • Grade 1 • Book 2

▶ **Read about the dog. Circle the word that completes each sentence. Then write the word.**

I have a dog. She is called Meg.
Meg is black. She can jump. She is fat.
My dog is soft. I am glad I have Meg.

dog   cat

_____
----

1. Meg is a _____.

_____

jog   jump

_____
----

2. Meg can _____.

_____

fat   thin

_____
----

3. Meg is _____.

_____

sick   soft

_____
----

4. Meg is _____.

School–Home Connection

Have your child read the story aloud. Then ask
your child to underline the words that give
details about the dog.

13

▶ **Write sk, sl, sp, st, or sw to complete each word.**

1. Jack ___**SW**___ am in the pond.

2. Todd _____ips on the path.

3. The dog has a _____ick.

4. Jim _____ills the milk.

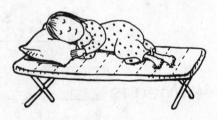

5. Beth _____ept on a cot.

14

Extra Support

© Harcourt • Grade 1 • Book 2

▶ **Write the word from the box that names each picture.**

bus	nut	cup
run	bug	hug

1.

bug

2.

3.

4.

5.

6.

16

Extra Support
© Harcourt • Grade 1 • Book 2

▶ **Say the name of each picture. Write u only if the name has the same u sound as in duck.**

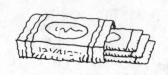

1. duck

2. g ___ m

3. l ___ g

4. t ___ b

5. s ___ n

6. b ___ ll

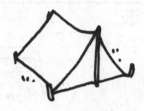

7. st ___ mp

8. sk ___ nk

9. t ___ nt

School–Home Connection

Point to each picture and ask your child to say the name. Then have him or her copy the words with *u* onto a separate sheet of paper.

18

Extra Support
© Harcourt • Grade 1 • Book 2

Name _____

▶ **Write the word that best completes each sentence.**

live   lift   like

_____

- - - - - - - - - - - - - -

1. A plant can _____ in a pot.

_____

got   grow   glass

_____

- - - - - - - - - - - - - -

2. Water helps it _____ tall.

_____

dust   dock   does

_____

- - - - - - - - - - - - - -

3. It wilts if it _____ not get water.

_____

Mend   Map   Many

_____

- - - - - - - - - - - - - -

4. _____ bugs like that plant.

_____

food   fond   flock

_____

- - - - - - - - - - - - - -

5. They think it's good _____.

Extra Support

© Harcourt • Grade 1 • Book 2

▶ **Read about the plant. Circle the word or words that complete each sentence correctly. Then write the word or words.**

   I have a plant. It is in a pot. The pot is black. The plant has a tall stem. There are two buds on the stem. The buds are pink. They are soft buds.

(a pot)   the mud

1. My plant is in 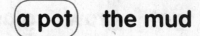  _____.

small   tall

2. The stem is _____.

Two buds   Some fuzz

3. _____ grow on the stem.

pink   red

4. The buds are _____.

 School–Home Connection

Have your child read the paragraph about the plant. Then have your child describe details about the plant.

20

Name _____

▶ **Write cr, dr, gr, or tr to complete each word.**

1. Ken is a ___cr___ab.

2. He can _____ink a glass of water.

3. One day, Ken _____ops his glass.

4. Ken thinks. Then he _____ins.

5. The _____ick is to drink as he runs.

 21

▶ **Say the name of each picture. Write ng if the word has the /ng/ sound, as in sing.**

1.

ring

2.

ki

3.

do

4.

swi

5.

ba

6.

wi

7.

fro

8.

bu

9.

so

🚒 **School–Home Connection**

Help your child think of words that rhyme with
the words that he or she completed.

23

Extra Support
© Harcourt • Grade 1 • Book 2

Name _____

► **Circle the word that completes each sentence. Then write the word.**

hang   hug

_____

- - - - - - - - - - - - - - -

1. I will _____ up the plant.

log   long

_____

- - - - - - - - - - - - - - -

2. This dress is too _____.

stump   stung

_____

- - - - - - - - - - - - - - -

3. Greg does not want to get _____.

swung   swum

_____

- - - - - - - - - - - - - - -

4. Meg _____ the bat.

bends   bangs

_____

- - - - - - - - - - - - - - -

5. Frank _____ on the drums.

School–Home Connection

Write the word pairs *bag* and *bang*, *thin* and *thing*, *sun* and *sung*. Have your child read each pair aloud. Talk about how the two words are alike and how they are different.

25

▶ **Circle the word that completes
each sentence.**

school   skill   small

1. We sing at _____.

_____

your   my   you

2. Now clap _____ hands.

_____

use   way   was

3. Mr. Cobb likes us to sing this _____.

_____

and   back   arms

4. Jen swings her _____.

_____

head   felt   feet

5. Tim taps his _____.

_____

all   two   every

6. We sing _____ song.

School–Home Connection

Have your child read each sentence aloud with
the correct word. Talk about why this word
is the best choice. Then ask your child to use
head and *use* in sentences.

26

Name _____

▶ **Read the story. Then circle each sentence that tells what happens.**

It was a hot day. Stan asked Dad to swim with him. Dad said he had a lot to do.

Mom said, "We can help you. Then you will have time to swim."

"Yes," said Dad. "I like that plan." That day, they all went to swim.

1. Stan wants to swim.

Stan wants to go to bed.

_____

2. Dad will go for a run.

Dad has a lot to do.

_____

3. Mom sits in the grass.

Mom and Stan help Dad.

_____

4. They all go to swim.

They all go to eat.

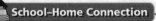
School–Home Connection

Look at the pictures and read the story with your child. Talk about what happens in the story. Have your child tell what happens at the end.

27

▶ **Read the chart. Write the contraction that completes each sentence.**

I will = I'll	They will = They'll
He will = He'll	It will = It'll

1. My cat is sick. _____I'll_____ call the vet.

2. _____ bring a gift.

3. _____ ring the bell.

4. _____ melt in the sun.

Extra Support
© Harcourt • Grade 1 • Book 2

▶ **Look at each picture. Circle the word that names the picture.**

I. 	**2.** 	**3.** 
store stork stop	corn cost horn	frost fort forest
4. 	**5.**	**6.**
cord core cross	for fork frog	hop corn horn
7. 	**8.** 	**9.** 
thorn storm trot	stop store storm	sport spot sort

30

Extra Support
© Harcourt • Grade 1 • Book 2

Name _____

▶ **Circle the word that completes each sentence. Then write the word.**

Corn   Crib

_____

1. _____ is food.

sport   fork

_____

2. Hank lifts his _____ .

milking   morning

_____

3. I get up in the _____ .

thorns   store

_____

4. This plant has _____ .

frog   forest

_____

5. The fox runs in the _____ .

 School–Home Connection

Ask your child to point to and read the words
that have the *or* sound, as in *sort* or *more*.

32

Extra Support
© Harcourt • Grade 1 • Book 2

▶ **Circle the word that completes the sentence. Then write the word.**

fish   has   from

_____

- - - - - - - - - - - - - - - - - - -

1. I have a pet _____.

_____

until   under   very

_____

- - - - - - - - - - - - - - - - - - -

2. He swims _____ the water.

_____

cold   their   kept

_____

- - - - - - - - - - - - - - - - - - -

3. The water is not too _____.

_____

under   animals   asked

_____

- - - - - - - - - - - - - - - - - - -

4. We have pet _____.

_____

vest   their   very

_____

- - - - - - - - - - - - - - - - - - -

5. The rabbit is _____ soft.

School–Home Connection

Have your child read each word choice and sentence aloud. Ask why he or she chose each word.

33

Extra Support

▶ **In the first group, circle the things that are for a man. In the second group, circle the things that are for a dog.**

man

dog

School–Home Connection

Ask your child to use pairs of pictured items in sentences about what a man and a dog would do. For example: *A man sleeps in a bed, but a dog sleeps in a dog bed.*

Extra Support
© Harcourt • Grade 1 • Book 2

▶ **Put together the two words. Write the new word.**

bath ⊂ ⊂ tub

sun ⊂ ⊂ set

1. _____

2. _____

pop ⊂ ⊂ corn

kick ⊂ ⊂ ball

3. _____

4. _____

ant ⊂ ⊂ hill

back ⊂ ⊂ pack

5. _____

6. _____

Extra Support
© Harcourt • Grade 1 • Book 2

▶ **Write the word from the box that names the picture.**

ship	cash	shed	fish	shell	dish

1.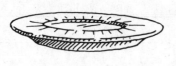

_____

- - - - - - - - - - - -

_____

2.

_____

- - - - - - - - - - - -

_____

3.

_____

- - - - - - - - - - - -

_____

4.

_____

- - - - - - - - - - - -

_____

5.

_____

- - - - - - - - - - - -

_____

6.

_____

- - - - - - - - - - - -

_____

Extra Support
© Harcourt • Grade 1 • Book 2

▶ **Read each sentence. Circle the word that has the /sh/ sound, as in ship. Write the word on the line.**

_____

1. I _____ I had a yak.

wish

think

_____

2. I could _____ his corn.

pick

mash

3. The yak could nap in

_____

the _____.

shack

hut

4. Yaks are not

_____

_____.

tall

short

5. I have a little

_____

_____.

gift

cash

_____

6. I will _____ for a yak.

shop

ask

School–Home Connection

Ask your child to read aloud the words he or she circled. Together, think of other words with the *sh* sound, as in *ship* and *fish*.

39

Extra Support
© Harcourt • Grade 1 • Book 2

▶ **Write the word that completes the
sentence.**

gold   gum   go

_____

- - - - - - - - - - - - - - - - -

I. Beth got a _____ ring.

head   happy   night

_____

- - - - - - - - - - - - - - - - -

2. Beth was _____.

saw   crash   came

_____

- - - - - - - - - - - - - - - - -

3. Bill _____ to look.

Could   Cord   Come

"_____

- - - - - - - - - - - - - - - - -

4. _____ I hold it?"

were   made   met

_____

- - - - - - - - - - - - - - - - -

5. The ring was _____ for Beth.

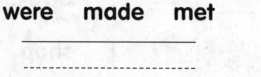

School–Home Connection

Ask your child to read each sentence with the
correct word. Talk about why the chosen word
is the only choice that fits in the sentence.

40

Name _____

▶ **Read the sentences. Draw a line from the sentences to the picture that shows the setting.**

1. We had a math test. The class did well. Miss Hill said, "Good job!"

2. Russ has fun in the sun. He digs in the sand. He swims in the water.

3. Dad planted corn. I fed the pig. Mom got eggs from the hen.

 School–Home Connection

Take turns with your child, pointing to pictures on the page. Talk about each place and about what could happen in that setting.

Extra Support
© Harcourt • Grade 1 • Book 2

▶ **Write cl, dr, fl, st, or sw to complete each word.**

1. Brad looks at the __cl__ock.

2. He will have to _____im fast.

3. He swims to the _____ag.

4. Brad _____ops at the flag.

5. He wants a _____ink of water.

School–Home Connection

Help your child read the sentences aloud.
Together, think of other words that begin with
cl, dr, fl, st, or *sw.*

Extra Support
© Harcourt • Grade 1 • Book 2

Reach for the Stars

Book 1-3

▶ **Say the name of each picture. If it has the sound of <u>ch</u>, as in <u>chick</u>, trace <u>ch</u>. If it does not, cross out <u>ch</u>.**

1.

ch

2.

ch

3.

ch

4.

ch

5.

ch

6.

ch

7.

ch

8.

ch

9.

ch

School–Home Connection

Ask which words have the same sound as the beginning sound in *chick*. As your child says the name of each picture, ask if the *ch* is at the beginning or end of the word.

2

▶ **Write the word from the box that names each picture.**

patch	watch	chin
catch	chest	lunch

1.

_____

- - - - - - - - - -

_____

2.

_____

- - - - - - - - - -

_____

3.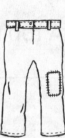

_____

- - - - - - - - - -

_____

4.

_____

- - - - - - - - - -

_____

5.

_____

- - - - - - - - - -

_____

6.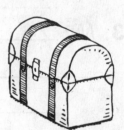

_____

- - - - - - - - - -

_____

▶ **Write a word from the box to complete each sentence.**

air	fly	friends	grew
need	play	rain	watch

1. A robin can _____.

2. It can go fast in the _____.

3. My _____ and I see a robin.

4. We _____ it make a nest.

5. The robin will _____ to rest.

🚌 **School–Home Connection**

Ask your child to read each sentence with you.
Then point to the word *grew* in the box, and
have your child think of a sentence using that
word. Repeat with *play* and *rain*.

5

▶ **Write 1, 2, and 3 to put the pictures in order. The first one is done.**

_____|_____   _____   _____
- - - - - - - | - - - - - - -   - - - - - - - - - - - - -   - - - - - - - - - - - - -
_____|_____   _____   _____

▶ **Draw a picture to show what might happen next.**

🚌 **School–Home Connection**

Ask your child to tell what is happening in
each picture. Talk about the correct order.
Then have your child explain the picture he or
she drew.

Extra Support
© Harcourt • Grade 1 • Book 3

▶ **Read the chart. Then write the word with <u>es</u> that completes each sentence.**

brush + es	brushes
dish + es	dishes
fix + es	fixes
match + es	matches
toss + es	tosses

1. Mr. York _____ fixes _____ the sink.

2. Her dress _____ her socks.

3. Chuck _____ the ball.

4. Ellen has two _____.

5. Fred will get the _____.

School–Home Connection

Have your child read aloud one of the sentences he or she completed. Ask what letters were added to the word. *(es)*

7

Name _____

▶ **Look at each picture. Circle the word that names the picture.**

1.

(barn)   ban   born

2.

far   form   farm

3.

shore   shark   shack

4.

scat   score   scarf

5.

yarn   yam   york

6.

am   arm   are

7.

car   core   cord

8.

much   more   march

9.

cat   cart   core

 School–Home Connection

Have your child read each word and point
to the letters that stand for the *ar* sound.
Ask your child to say a sentence about each
picture, using the word he or she circled.

9

Extra Support
© Harcourt • Grade 1 • Book 3

▶ **Circle the word that completes each sentence. Then write the word.**

card   cord
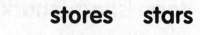
_____

----

1. I got a _____.

stores   stars

----

2. I see _____ up there.

for   far

----

3. Brad ran very _____.

park   pork

----

4. She will _____ the van.

born   barn

----

5. The _____ is on a hill.

School–Home Connection

Help your child read each completed sentence aloud. Talk about how the word choices are alike and how they are different.

11

Extra Support
© Harcourt • Grade 1 • Book 3

▶ **Write a word from the box to complete each sentence.**

again	feel	house	know
loud	Mrs.	put	say

_____

1. I ran out of the _____.

_____

2. _____ Hall is in her yard.

_____

3. I _____ she didn't see me.

_____

4. I _____ good morning.

_____

5. She _____ on her hat.

School-Home Connection

Have your child read each word from the
box. Help him or her to read each completed
sentence aloud.

Extra Support
© Harcourt • Grade 1 • Book 3

Name _____

Read the story. Circle the sentence and picture that tells why the author wrote it. Then circle the best answer to the question.

Helping Lost Pets

by Liz Smith

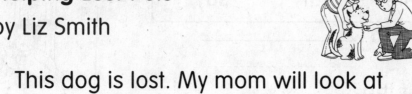

This dog is lost. My mom will look at its tag. Now Mom knows who to call. A tag can help lost pets get home.

1. Liz Smith wants us to get a dog.

Liz Smith wants us to know how to help lost pets.

Liz Smith wants us to have fun.

2. Who is telling this?

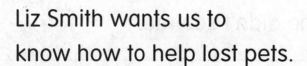

School–Home Connection

Help your child read the story aloud. Talk about the pictures. Then ask your child to tell why he or she chose each answer.

13

Extra Support
© Harcourt • Grade 1 • Book 3

▶ **Read the chart. Then write the word with -s, -ed, or -ing that completes each sentence.**

fish	-ing	fishing
check	-ed	checked
grill	-ed	grilled
help	-s	helps
itch	-ing	itching

_____
----

1. Dad and I are _____.

_____
----

2. Dad _____ his rod for fish.

_____
----

3. Pam _____ some food.

_____
----

4. Brett _____ set up the tent.

_____
----

5. His arm was _____ a lot.

School–Home Connection

Have your child read aloud one of the sentences he or she completed. Ask how the word in the box changed.

Extra Support
© Harcourt • Grade 1 • Book 3

▶ **Circle the word that completes the sentence. Then write the word.**

quilt   whiz

_____

- -

1. The _____ on my bed is soft.

whip   quit

_____

- -

2. The man _____ fishing.

When   Quit

_____

- -

3. _____ can we go out?

which   quick

_____

- -

4. The dogs are _____.

whacks   quacks

_____

- -

5. The duck _____.

🚌 **School–Home Connection**

Point to the words *whacks* and *quacks*. Talk
about how the words are alike and different.

16

▶ **Write <u>qu</u> or <u>wh</u> to complete each word.**

_____
- - - - - - - - -
1. Meg has a math _____iz.

_____
- - - - - - - -
2. _____ich one is my gift?

_____
- - - - - - - - -
3. This is my _____ilt.

_____
- - - - - - -
4. "_____ack!" said the duck.

_____
- - - - - - - -
5. Sam cried _____en he fell.

School–Home Connection

Have your child read each sentence aloud.
Work together to think of other words that
begin with the sounds of *wh* and *qu*.

18

▶ **Write a word from the box to complete each sentence.**

about	books	family	name
people	read	work	writing

1. Carl has two _____.

2. Mark is _____.

3. Beth can _____ to the class.

4. Fred tells _____ his trip.

Marvin

5. Marvin prints his _____.

6. Chuck does his _____.

School–Home Connection

Have your child read each word in the box aloud. Then ask your child to read each sentence to you.

19

▶ **Write 1, 2, and 3 to put the pictures in
order. Then write the sentences in order.
The first one has been done for you.**

_____ Last, a chick comes out of the egg.

_1_ First, a hen sits on her egg.

_____ Next, the egg hatches.

1. _____

2. _____

3. _____

School–Home Connection

Ask your child to tell what is happening in
each picture. Help your child use the words
first, *next*, and *last*.

20

Extra Support
© Harcourt • Grade 1 • Book 3

Name _____

Phonics: Inflections
-ed, -ing
(double final
consonant)
Lesson 15

▶ **Put together the root word and the word ending. Then write the new word. Remember to double the final letter of the root word.**

stop ⊂ ⊂ ed

stop ⊂ ⊂ ing

1. _____

2. _____

clip ⊂ ⊂ ed

clip ⊂ ⊂ ing

3. _____

4. _____

mop ⊂ ⊂ ed

mop ⊂ ⊂ ing

5. _____

6. _____

School–Home Connection

Write the words *clap, clapped,* and *clapping.*
Ask your child to tell how the word *clap*
changes when *-ed* and *-ing* are added.

21

Name _____

▶ **Circle the word that names the picture.**

1.	**2.**	**3.**
bird bud bring	clerk card curl	grill girl gift
4.	**5.**	**6.**
skin skirt scarf	fern fist first	dirt dart drip
7.	**8.**	**9.**
star stir store	third think tent	barn born burn

23

Name _____

Phonics:
r-Controlled
Vowels
/ûr/*er, ir, ur*

Lesson 16

▶ **Write a word from the box to name each picture.**

fern	shirt	curb
fur	turnip	hurt

1.

_____

- - - - - - - - - - - - - - - -

_____

2.

_____

- - - - - - - - - - - - - - - -

_____

3.

_____

- - - - - - - - - - - - - - - -

_____

4.

_____

- - - - - - - - - - - - - - - -

_____

5.

_____

- - - - - - - - - - - - - - - -

_____

6.

_____

- - - - - - - - - - - - - - - -

_____

School–Home Connection

Have your child read each word aloud. Write the words *her*, *girl*, and *turn*. Ask your child to circle the letters that make the same sound in each word. (*er, ir, ur*)

25

▶ **Write a word from the box to
complete each sentence.**

always	by	Cow's	join
nice	Please	room	

_____
----

1. Bird went to _____ his friends.

_____
----

2. "Is there _____ for me?"

_____
----

3. "Yes. _____ sit with us."

_____
----

4. Bird _____ sits by Hen.

_____
----

5. Hen is very _____.

School–Home Connection

Point to the word *Cow's* in the box, and ask
your child to read it. Have your child use the
word in a sentence about something that
belongs to a cow.

Extra Support
© Harcourt • Grade 1 • Book 3

Name _____

► **Circle the sentence that tells what the picture is about.**

1.

The birds can chirp.

The birds have a bath.

2.

They all ran a long way.

The ostrich came in first.

3.

Rabbit went to the market.

Rabbit will go home.

4.

Jack has a good book.

They like to stand up.

5.

I have a big yard to play in.

There's a skunk in my yard!

6.

Dan forgot his lunch.

Friends sit on a bench.

School–Home Connection

Talk about what is happening in each picture.
Pretend that each picture is the cover of a
book. Together, think of a good title for each
one that tells what the story is about.

27

Extra Support
© Harcourt • Grade 1 • Book 3

▶ **Look at the picture. Add <u>er</u> or <u>est</u> to each word. Write the word in the sentence.**

small

_____

- -

1. The frog is the _____ animal.

_____

fast

_____

- -

2. A fox is _____ than a frog.

_____

soft

_____

- -

3. A cat's fur is _____ than a fox's.

_____

smart

_____

- -

4. I am the _____ of all.

School–Home Connection

Write the words *big*, *bigger*, and *biggest*. Have your child draw a picture of three animals and label each animal with one of the words.

28

▶ **Circle the word that names the picture.**

1. 	2. 	3.
(bottle) battle bundle	tattle turnip turtle	cuddle candle garden
4. 	5. 	6. 
cattle kettle little	rattle radish ruffle	ankle antler apple
7. 	8. 	9. 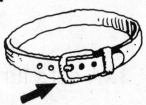
freckle fiddle fitted	purple puffin puddle	buckle bucket bubble

School–Home Connection

Have your child find and read the words that
end in -*le*. Ask him or her to choose two of
the words and write them on a separate sheet
of paper.

Name _____

▶ **Write the word from the box that names the picture.**

ankle	turtle	bubble
juggle	pickle	paddle

1.

_____

- -

_____

2.

_____

- -

_____

3.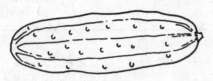

_____

- -

_____

4.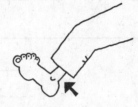

_____

- -

_____

5.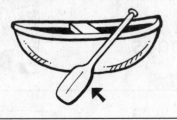

_____

- -

_____

6.

_____

- -

_____

School–Home Connection

Have your child practice writing these words that end in -*le*: *cuddle*, *little*, *giggle*, and *startle*.

32

▶ **Write a word from the box to complete each sentence.**

buy	carry	money	other
paint	paper	would	

_____
- - - - - - - - - - - - - - - - - -
1. Mom has the _____ .

_____
- - - - - - - - - - - - - - - - - -
2. Pam will _____ brushes.

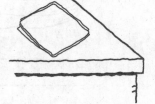

_____
- - - - - - - - - - - - - - - - - -
3. She will get _____ , too.

_____
- - - - - - - - - - - - - - - - - -
4. We _____ the bags.

_____
- - - - - - - - - - - - - - - - - -
5. Pam will _____ animals.

School–Home Connection
Have your child read each word in the box. Ask
him or her to use each word in a sentence.

33

Extra Support
© Harcourt • Grade 1 • Book 3

Name _____

▶ **Look at the pictures and read the sentences. Then circle the sentence that tells what this is mainly about.**

You can find
fish in ponds.

Frogs hatch from
eggs in ponds.

Some insects
live in ponds.

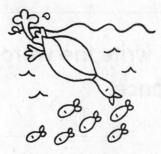

Ducks hunt for
food in ponds.

- **Ducks have to hunt in ponds.**
- **Many animals live in ponds.**
- **Insects live in ponds.**

School–Home Connection

Have your child read the sentences. Talk about
the pictures and the main idea. Together, think
of a good title for this information story.

34

► **Trace the words that have <u>ed</u> and <u>ing</u> added to them. Then read the chart.**

	ed	ing
1. hop	hopped	hopping
2. nap	napped	napping
3. mop	mopped	mopping

► **Now write the word from the chart that completes the sentence.**

4. I am _____ like a frog.

5. I _____ up the water.

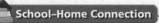
School–Home Connection

Write the words *zipped* and *dripping*. Ask
your child to read each word and say it in a
sentence.

35

Extra Support
© Harcourt • Grade 1 • Book 3

▶ **Circle the word that names the picture. Then write the word.**

1.

box

----

bow

2.

got

----

goat

3.

boat

----

bat

4.

toast

----

test

5.

mop

----

mow

6.

soap

----

stop

7.

cot

----

coat

8.

rod

----

road

School–Home Connection

Write the words *row* and *boat*. Help your child read the words. Then ask which letters in the words make the long o sound, as in *go*. (*ow* and *oa*)

37

▶ **Write the word from the box that names the picture.**

toad	snow	bowl
road	crow	coat

1.

_____
- - - - - - - - - - - -
_____

2.

_____
- - - - - - - - - - - -
_____

3.

_____
- - - - - - - - - - - -
_____

4.

_____
- - - - - - - - - - - -
_____

5.

_____
- - - - - - - - - - - -
_____

6.

_____
- - - - - - - - - - - -
_____

School–Home Connection

Have your child read each word aloud. Talk about how the words are alike and how they are different.

39

Extra Support
© Harcourt • Grade 1 • Book 3

Name _____

▶ **Write a word from the box to complete the sentence.**

mouse	our	over
pretty	surprise	three

_____

1. Can Jan come to _____ house?

2. Jan can come _____ to play.

3. We play with _____ dolls.

4. I have a _____ for Jan.

5. It's a stuffed _____.

School–Home Connection

Play a memory game. Write each word from the box on two slips of paper or cards. Turn each word face down. Have your child find matching pairs by turning over two cards at a time and reading them.

40

Extra Support
© Harcourt • Grade 1 • Book 3

Name _____

▶ **Read the sentences. Then circle the sentence that tells why the author wrote the story.**

What Plants Need
by Brent Hall

Good dirt helps a plant grow.

A plant needs water to live.

A plant needs sun, too.

With all these things, a plant can grow.

- Brent Hall wants us to know about the sun.

- Brent Hall wants us to know about dirt.

- Brent Hall wants us to know what plants need to grow.

School–Home Connection

Have your child read the sentences to you. Talk about how the author probably feels about plants. Ask, "Why do you think the author wrote about plants?"

Extra Support
© Harcourt • Grade 1 • Book 3

Name _____

▶ **Circle the word that completes the sentence. Then write the word.**

grown   glow

_____
- -

1. Ann has _____.

row   roast

_____
- -

2. We _____ hot dogs.

thrown   throat

_____
- -

3. I have _____ the ball.

oat   own

_____
- -

4. She has her _____ doll.

coast   cost

_____
- -

5. We went to the _____.

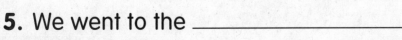

School–Home Connection

Have your child read each completed sentence aloud. Talk about how the word choices in each set are alike and how they are different.

42

Make Your Mark

Book 1-4

▶ **Circle the word that names the picture.**

1.

beans bins buns

2.

eat egg eagle

3.

they three throw

4.

teeth toad team

5.

feet fit fast

6.

ship she shell

7.

job jet jeep

8.

lift leaf loft

9.

needle nod
neat

School–Home Connection

Have your child find all the words that have
the long e sound, as in *bean*.

2

Extra Support
© Harcourt • Grade 1 • Book 4

▶ **Circle the word that names the picture.**
Then write the word.

1.

_____

 tree

(tree)
tray

2.

_____

_____

jeans
just

3.

_____

_____

leak
lick

4.

_____

_____

end
eat

5.

_____

_____

patch
peach

6.

_____

_____

quiz
queen

7.

_____

_____

seed
said

8.

_____

_____

ship
sheep

School–Home Connection

Ask your child to read aloud the words that
have the letters *ee*. Repeat this activity for the
words that have the letters *ea*.

4

▶ **Write the word that completes each sentence.**

_____
----

1. Dean and his _____ go out.

   door   mother

_____
----

2. Mom locks the _____.

   hurry   door

_____
----

3. They _____ to the park.

   dear   hurry

_____
----

4. The sun is in the _____.

   should   sky

_____
----

5. Dean _____ have fun.

   should   told

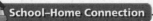
School–Home Connection

Have your child read each sentence aloud.
Together, think of other sentences for the
words he or she chose from.

5

► **Look at the picture that shows what happened. Then circle the sentence that tells why it happened.**

What Happened?	Why Did It Happen?
1.	She dropped the cup. She is sad.
2.	He is nice. He is sick.
3.	The sun melted the snow. The snow is cold.
4.	They are sitting. They like the play.

School–Home Connection

Point to each picture, and ask your child to tell what happened. Then have your child explain why it happened.

6

Name _____

▶ **Write the word that completes each
sentence.**

_____
- -

1. _____ clapped my hands.

I've
We've

_____
_____
- -

2. _____ going to the park.

They've
They're

_____
_____
- -

3. _____ had so much fun.

We've
We're

_____
_____
- -

4. _____ my good friend.

You're
You've

_____
_____
- -

5. _____ hopping and skipping.

I've
We're

Extra Support
© Harcourt • Grade 1 • Book 4

▶ **Circle the word that names the picture.**

1.

hay   hat   hit

2.

stun   stain   stand

3.

rain   ran   run

4.

pan   pain   paint

5.

plain   play   plan

6.

tray   tan   tree

7.

trot   tan   train

8.

can   chain   chin

9.

pay   pail   pan

**School–Home Connection**

Ask your child to point to the words with the
long *a* sound spelled with *ai*, as in *main*. Then ask
him or her to point to the words with the long *a*
sound spelled with *ay*, as in *say*.

9

► **Circle the word that completes the sentence. Then write the word.**

nails   nests

_____

- - - - - - - - - - - - - - - - - -

1. Lee buys a box of _____.

_____

dart   day

_____

- - - - - - - - - - - - - - - - -

2. It is a hot _____.

_____

plop   play

_____

- - - - - - - - - - - - - - - -

3. The girls _____ with blocks.

_____

rain   rays

_____

- - - - - - - - - - - - - - - -

4. Jay can't go out in the _____.

_____

brands   braids

_____

- - - - - - - - - - - - - - - -

5. Kathleen likes her _____.

Extra Support
© Harcourt • Grade 1 • Book 4

Name _____

▶ **Circle the word that completes the sentence. Then write the word.**

warm   move
_____
- - - - - - - - - - - - - - - - - -

I. My jacket keeps me _____.

_____

four   dry
_____
- - - - - - - - - - - - - - - - - -

2. My raincoat keeps me _____.

_____

cool   place
_____
- - - - - - - - - - - - - - - - - -

3. Shorts keep me _____ in the summer.

_____

holes   place
_____
- - - - - - - - - - - - - - - - - -

4. I live in a nice _____.

_____

warm   holes
_____
- - - - - - - - - - - - - - - - - -

5. I dig _____ in the sand each day.

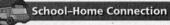
School–Home Connection

Have your child use one of the words he or she
wrote in a sentence to tell something about
the area in which you live.

12

Name ______________________________

Comprehension: Cause and Effect
Lesson 20

▶ **The picture shows what is happening. Circle the sentence that tells why it is happening.**

What Is Happening?	Why Is It Happening?
1. 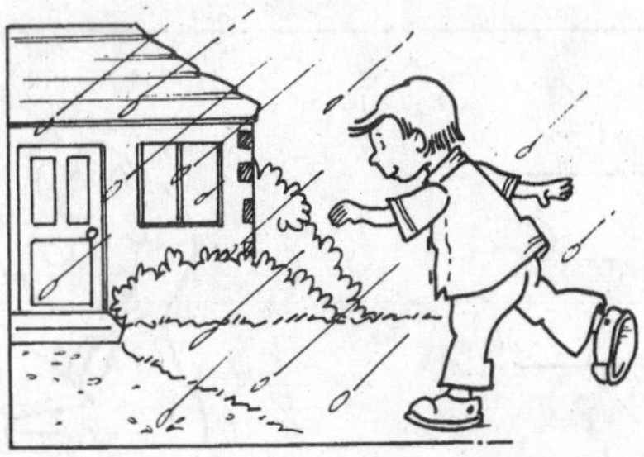	It is raining. His name is Jack.
2. 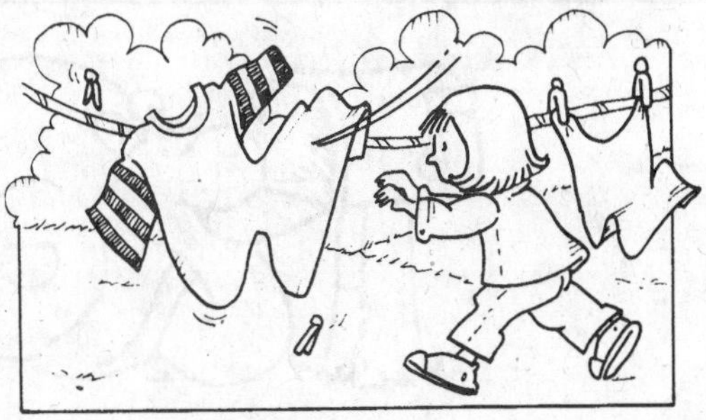	The wind is blowing hard. The dress is nice.
3. 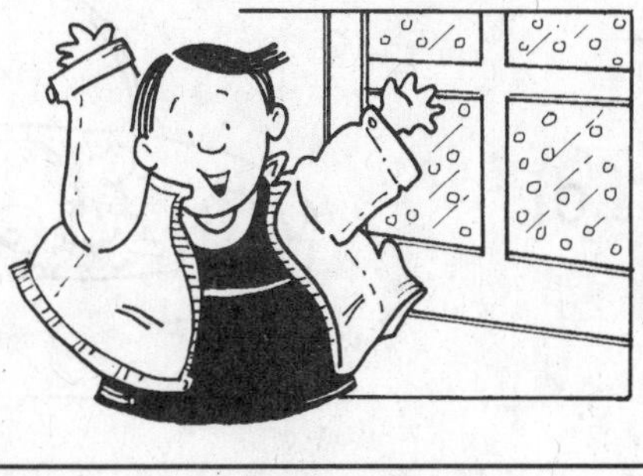	He looks good. It is cold outside.
4. 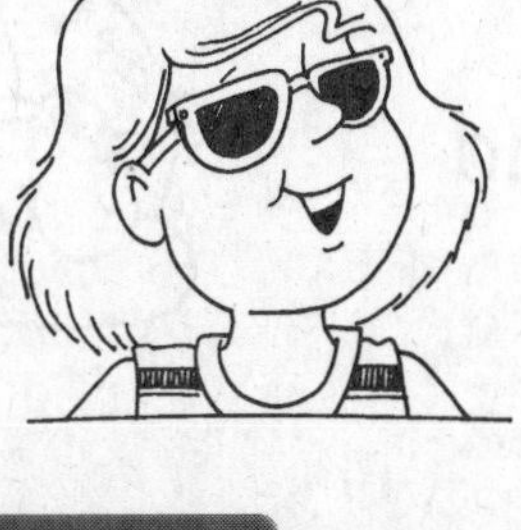	The sun is very bright. She likes to play.

School-Home Connection

Have your child tell what is happening in each picture. Then ask him or her why this might be happening.

▶ **Write ail or aid to complete the word.**

1. Ben is a __sn_____.

2. Ben's boat has a __s_____.

3. He got his __m_____.

4. He swam in a __p_____ of water.

5. Then Ben __l_____ his head down.

School–Home Connection

Have your child read the words he or she completed in the sentences. Together, think of other words that end in *ail* or *aid*.

14

▶ **Say the name of each picture. Write a only if the name has the long a sound, as in vase.**

1.

v a s e

2.

c   c   k e

3.

c   p

4.

g r   p e

5.

c   v e

6.

c   t

7.

r   k e

8.

l   l   k e

9.

c   n

🚌 **School–Home Connection**

Write the words *ate, plate,* and *taste.* Have your
child read each word, draw a picture for it, and
label the picture.

16

Extra Support
© Harcourt • Grade 1 • Book 4

▶ **Circle the word that names the picture.**

1.

(cape) cap cup

2.

plan pin plane

3.

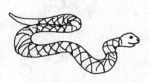

lock lake lick

4.

rack rock rake

5.

skate skit scat

6.

snap snake sell

7.

tip tap tape

8.

plot plate pat

9.

wall whale will

School–Home Connection

Write the words *ape*, *wave*, and *chase*. Ask
your child to read each word, draw a picture
for it, and label the picture.

18

Extra Support
© Harcourt • Grade 1 • Book 4

Name ______________________

Choose the word that completes each sentence.

1. Snake __________ a loud crash.

hears **might**

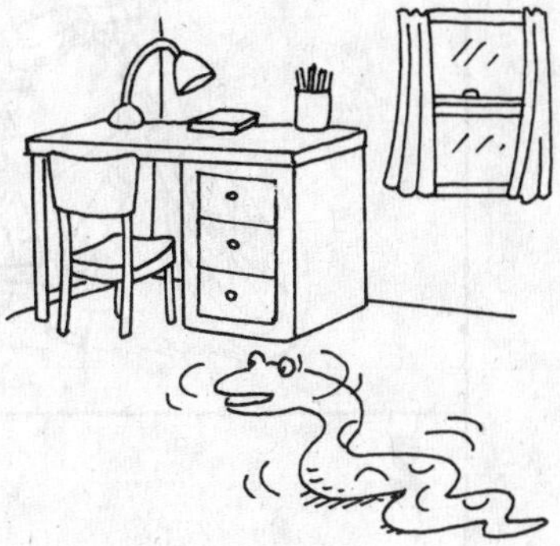

2. Snake looks __________.

open **around**

3. He checks __________ the desk.

near **gone**

4. He looks by the __________ door.

tired **open**

5. Snake has __________ spilled paint.

might **found**

School–Home Connection

Have your child read each completed sentence aloud. Point to the word *gone* under Sentence 3, and have your child use it in a sentence.

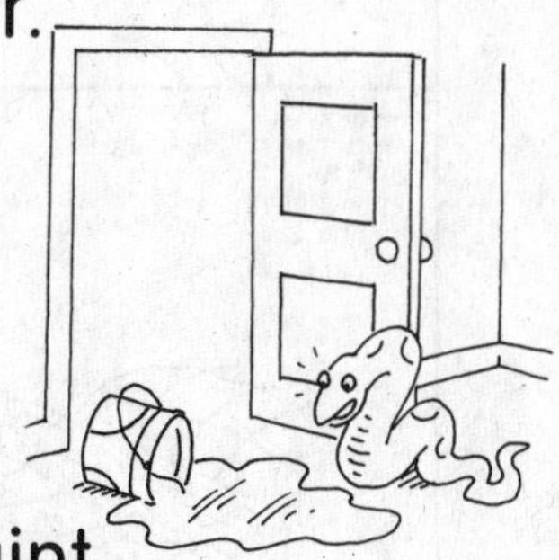

Name _____

▶ **Draw a line from the problem to the solution.**

School–Home Connection

Talk about each picture with your child. Ask
your child to describe each problem and its
solution.

Extra Support
© Harcourt • Grade 1 • Book 4

Name _____

▶ **Write <u>ane</u> or <u>ade</u> to complete each word.**

1. Shane has a __cane__.

2. He __m_____ a cake.

3. Shane got on a __pl____.

4. Shane was very happy to see __J____.

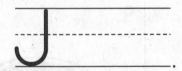

5. Jane was glad __Sh____ came.

🚌 **School–Home Connection**

Ask your child to read the completed sentences
aloud. Write the word *trade.* Have your
child read the word and then draw a picture
of Shane trading something with Jane.

21

▶ Circle the word that names the picture.

1.

bit   bike   bake

2.

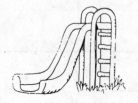

slit   sled   slide

3.

pine   pin   pane

4.

nip   name   nine

5.

fine   fire   first

6.

hive   his   time

7.

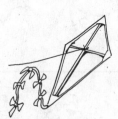

hike   kite   kit

8.

dim   dome   dime

9.

tire   tar   tore

School–Home Connection

Write the words *rip, ripe, pin, pine, bit,* and *bite*. Have your child read each word aloud.

Extra Support
© Harcourt • Grade 1 • Book 4

► **Circle the word that completes the sentence. Then write the word.**

dim   ⟨dime⟩

1. That will cost a __dime__ .

_____

rid   ride

2. I like to _____ my bike.

_____

bite   bit

3. I take a _____ of the apple.

_____

kit   kite

4. I can fly the _____ .

_____

shin   shine

5. The sun will _____ .

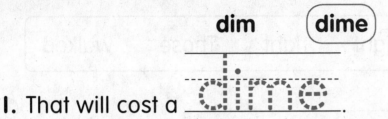
25

Extra Support
© Harcourt • Grade 1 • Book 4

Name _____

▶ **Write a word from the box to complete
each sentence.**

| because | light | right | Those | walked |

_____
- -

1. Duck _____ to the game.

_____
- - - - - - - - - - - - - - - - - - - -

2. The game started _____ away.

_____
- -

3. _____ players are good.

_____
- -

4. The bat was not _____.

_____
- -

5. Hen left _____ the game ended.

School–Home Connection

Ask your child to think about a favorite game.
Have your child use a word from the box to tell
something about the game.

26

▶ **The pictures show problems. Circle the sentence that tells the solution.**

1.

   He could get a backpack.

   He could eat lunch.

2.

   She could water the plant.

   She could put on a raincoat.

3.

   He could call his friends.

   He could take a nap.

27

▶ **Write the word with <u>-ed</u> or <u>-ing</u> that completes each sentence.**

smile	+	ing	=	smiling
skate	+	ing	=	skating
wave	+	ed	=	waved
pile	+	ing	=	piling
tire	+	ed	=	tired

_____
- -

1. Mike is very _____.

_____
- -

2. Mark is _____.

_____
- -

3. Chad _____ to me.

_____
- -

4. I will go _____.

🚌 **School–Home Connection**

Have your child read aloud the sentences he
or she completed. Ask how the words in the
box changed.

28

Extra Support
© Harcourt • Grade 1 • Book 4

▶ **Look at each picture. Circle the word that names the picture.**

1.

(globe) glow glob

2.

nice   nod   nose

3.

him   home   ham

4.

store   staff   stove

5.

rose   raise   roams

6.

smock   smoke
smug

7.

rob   rope   ripe

8.

house   hiss   hose

9.

note   not   night

30

▶ **Circle the word that completes each sentence. Then write the word.**

(**hope**) **hop**

_____

- - - - - - - - - - - - - - - - - -

1. "I _____ you like the gift."

not   **note**

_____

- - - - - - - - - - - - - - - - - -

2. Tom is reading a _____ .

rob   **robe**

_____

- - - - - - - - - - - - - - - - - -

3. Her _____ has birds on it.

stove   **bone**

_____

- - - - - - - - - - - - - - - - - -

4. Mom puts a pot on the _____ .

Rose   **Those**

_____

- - - - - - - - - - - - - - - - - -

5. _____ sheep are ours.

School–Home Connection

Have your child read each word choice aloud.
Together, make up sentences for the words
not used.

32

Name _____

▶ **Write the word that completes each sentence.**

city   pulled

_____

- - - - - - - - - - - - - - - -

1. I ride on a bus to the _____.

brown   hello

_____

- - - - - - - - - - - - - - - -

2. My mom says _____ to the driver.

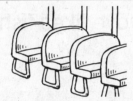

brown   loudly

_____

- - - - - - - - - - - - - - - -

3. The bus seats are green and _____.

love   loudly

_____

- - - - - - - - - - - - - - - -

4. Cars honk their horns _____.

hello   love

_____

- - - - - - - - - - - - - - - -

5. I _____ to look out the window.

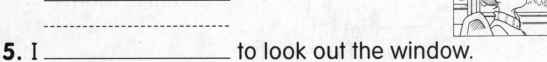

School–Home Connection

Talk with your child about things people might see and do in your neighborhood. Encourage him or her to use words from this page as you talk.

33

► **Look at the pictures, and read the clues. Draw a line around the sentence that draws a conclusion.**

1.

Kate is sitting.

Kate has a birthday.

2.

Dave likes to swim.

Dave likes fish.

3.

Rose wants to be a vet.

Rose wants to be an artist.

4.

He went to the store.

He is a nice man.

School–Home Connection

Ask your child to tell what clues are in the picture. Then have him or her read each sentence. Ask which sentence matches the picture.

34

▶ **Write <u>one</u> or <u>ole</u> to complete each word.**

1. Ruffles gets his b<u>one</u>.

2. Then he plays with a st_____.

3. Ruffles digs a h_____.

4. He jumps over a p_____.

5. Ruffles finds a c_____.

🚌 **School–Home Connection**

Have your child read each sentence aloud. Ask him or her to write each completed word on a separate sheet of paper.

35

Extra Support
© Harcourt • Grade 1 • Book 4

Name _____

Phonics:
Consonants /s/c;
/j/g, dge
• • • • • • • • • • •
Lesson 24

▶ **Write the word that names each picture. Choose from the box.**

circle	pencil	ice
stage	bridge	badge

1.

bridge

2.

_____

3.

_____

4.

_____

5.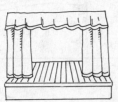

_____

6.

_____

School–Home Connection

Write the words *prince*, *large*, and *fudge*. Help
your child read each word aloud. Then ask him
or her to draw a picture for each word and
label it.

37

Name _____

Phonics:
Consonants /s/c;
/j/g, dge
Lesson 24

► **Choose the word that matches each clue.**

1.
    You must run fast in this.
    race   rake   rate

    _____
    ‑‑‑‑race‑‑‑‑

2.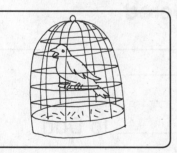
    You need a rocket to go there.
    spice   space   spike

    _____
    ‑‑‑‑‑‑‑‑‑‑‑‑‑‑‑

3.
    My bird stays in here.
    case   came   cage

    _____
    ‑‑‑‑‑‑‑‑‑‑‑‑‑‑‑
    _____

4. You can read this.
    page   pale   pace

    _____
    ‑‑‑‑‑‑‑‑‑‑‑‑‑‑‑

39

▶ **Write the word that completes the
sentence.**

1. The dog's _____ were on
   the cake.   **become   eyes**

2. Dad was with a _____.

   high   visitor

3. Dad likes to _____ with people.

   talk   remembered

4. I wanted to _____ to Dad.

   busy   listen

5. Then I _____
   the dog!   **talk   remembered**

School–Home Connection

Have your child read each completed
sentence aloud. Point to the word *high* under
Sentence 2 and ask your child to use the word
in a sentence.

40

▶ **Look at the pictures and the clues.
Circle the sentence that draws the
correct conclusion.**

1. Jan likes animals.

The hamster reads books.

2. It is a cold day.

It is a hot day.

3. Ned's cat is lost.

Ned does not like cats.

4. Meg is going to the beach.

It is Meg's birthday.

School–Home Connection

Ask your child to look at each picture and
describe the details he or she sees. Then have
your child read the sentence that describes the
picture.

41

Name _____

Phonics:
Contractions
's, n't, 'll
. . . .
Lesson 24

▶ **Choose the contraction that completes each sentence.**

1. ___**Ben's**___ going fishing.

   Ben's   **Didn't**

2. _____ at the lake now.

   He's   **He'll**

3. _____ eat a sandwich.

   They've   **He'll**

4. He _____ bring a drink.

   hasn't   **didn't**

5. Ben _____ catch fish while he sleeps.

   hasn't   **can't**

School–Home Connection

Have your child read each completed sentence aloud. Together, say the two words that make up each contraction.

42

Watch This!

Book 1-5

▶ **Say the name of each picture. Write u
only if the name has the long u sound,
as in cute or flute.**

1.

fl__te

2.

tr__ck

3.

h__g

4.

__t__b

5.

c__be

6.

t__be

7.

gr__pes

8.

m__le

9.

t__re

School–Home Connection

Ask your child to say each picture name. Have
him or her write the words with the long _u_
sound.

Extra Support
© Harcourt • Grade 1 • Book 5

▶ **Circle the word that completes the sentence. Then write the word.**

hug   huge

_____

- - - - - - - - - - - - - - - - -

1. That whale is _____.

mule   meal

_____

- - - - - - - - - - - - - - - - -

2. He has a _____.

flake   flute

_____

- - - - - - - - - - - - - - - - -

3. Jill plays the _____.

tin   tune

_____

- - - - - - - - - - - - - - - - -

4. I will play a _____.

cube   cub

_____

- - - - - - - - - - - - - - - - -

5. An ice _____ is in my glass.

▶ **Circle the word that completes the sentence. Then write the word.**

clear   kinds

_____

- -

1. The store has all _____ of pets.

color   hair

_____

- -

2. This cat has long _____.

clear   good-bye

_____

- -

3. The fish swims in a _____ tank.

color   toes

_____

- -

4. What _____ is that bird?

only   good-bye

_____

- -

5. I say _____ to the pets.

School–Home Connection

Have your child read each sentence aloud.
Encourage your child to write more sentences
about his or her favorite animals.

5

▶ **Find the word that comes <u>first</u> in ABC order. Fill in the circle in front of the word.**

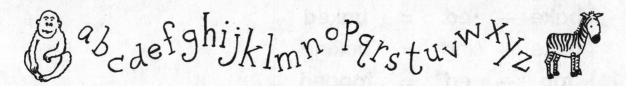

1. ○ eel   ○ flea   ● duck

2. ○ fish   ○ ape   ○ moth

3. ○ crane   ○ goat   ○ bee

4. ○ pig   ○ crow   ○ snake

5. ○ mule   ○ shark   ○ yak

6. ○ whale   ○ snail   ○ rat

7. ○ stork   ○ geese   ○ bird

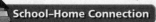
School–Home Connection

Help your child read each group of words aloud. Ask him or her to circle the names of four favorite animals and then write them in alphabetical order.

6

Name _____

▶ **Put together the word and the word ending. Then write the new word.**

bake	+	ed	=	baked
bake	+	ing	=	baking
tap	+	ed	=	tapped
tap	+	ing	=	tapping

wave ⊂ ⊃ ed   wave ⊂ ⊃ ing

1. _____   2. _____

tug ⊂ ⊃ ed   tug ⊂ ⊃ ing

3. _____   4. _____

use ⊂ ⊃ ed   use ⊂ ⊃ ing

5. _____   6. _____

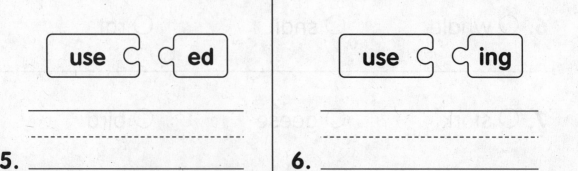

School–Home Connection

Have your child read each completed word to you. Talk about how each word changed when *ed* or *ing* was added.

7

▶ **Circle the word that names the picture.**

1. 	**2.** 	**3.** 
fly flip flow	pea pie pay	lit late light
4. 	**5.** 	**6.** 
free fly fry	tea tie fight	sky skip skate
7.	**8.** 	**9.** 
night next neat	kind crow cry	high hay hung

 School–Home Connection

Have your child name each picture and read
all three words aloud. Encourage your child to
write a sentence using a word he or she circled.

9

► **Circle the word that completes each sentence. Then write the word.**

(**dried**) deed

dried

1. I _____ the dishes.

_____

mitt   might

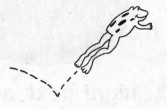

2. That book _____ fall down.

_____

try   tray

3. Frank will _____ to paint a boat.

_____

high   hay

4. A frog can jump _____ in the air.

11

▶ **Write the word that completes the sentence.**

climbed	earth

_____
_____

1. I wanted to read about the _____ .

_____

thought	fooling

_____
_____

2. I _____ I could find some books.

_____

climbed	earth

_____
_____

3. I _____ up high.

_____

table	fooling

_____
_____

4. The shelf was empty! Who was _____ me?

_____

earth	table

_____
_____

5. The books were right on the _____ .

Extra Support
© Harcourt • Grade 1 • Book 5

▶ **Read the story. Then circle the picture that answers each question.**

The sun shines on the creek. Beaver chops down a small tree. Soon he will have a new home.

Beaver hears children. Splash! He slaps his tail on the water to tell all the beavers to hide.

Chomp! Nibble! Beaver must hurry. The sun is setting. At last, Beaver has a home. He is happy.

1. Where does this story happen?

2. Who is this story about?

3. What happens at the end?

13

▶ **Write the contraction that completes the sentence.**

I'd   We'd

1. ___I'd___ play with you if I had a mitt.

I'd   They're

2. _____ painting the barn red.

You're   I've

3. _____ riding a nice bike, Tom.

We've   They're

4. _____ picked lots of apples.

Name _____

▶ **Write the word from the box that names the picture.**

cow	flower	owl
house	cloud	mouth

1.

_____

- - - - - - - - - - - - - - - -

_____

2.

_____

- - - - - - - - - - - - - - - -

_____

3.

_____

- - - - - - - - - - - - - - - -

_____

4.

_____

- - - - - - - - - - - - - - - -

_____

5.

_____

- - - - - - - - - - - - - - - -

_____

6.

_____

- - - - - - - - - - - - - - - -

_____

 16

▶ **Circle the word that completes the sentence. Then write the word.**

mouse   moss

_____

- - - - - - - - - - - - - - - - - - -

1. Dwight is a _____.

_____

out   oat

_____

- - - - - - - - - - - - - - - - - - -

2. He ran _____ of milk.

_____

couch   bench

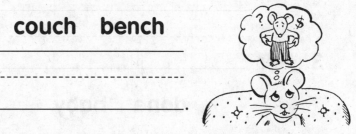

_____

- - - - - - - - - - - - - - - - - - -

3. Dwight sat on the _____.

_____

found   fond

_____

- - - - - - - - - - - - - - - - - - -

4. He _____ some money.

_____

hose   house

_____

- - - - - - - - - - - - - - - - - - -

5. Dwight left the _____.

School–Home Connection

Have your child read each completed sentence aloud. Talk about how the word choices are the same and how they are different.

18

Name _____

▶ **Choose a word to complete the sentence.**

_____
- -

1. Mrs. Brown _____ the door.

        answered   **together**

_____

_____
- -

2. We went to the park _____.

        heard   **together**

_____

_____
- -

3. Her _____ went with us.

        done   **baby**

_____

_____
- -

4. I _____ him in the swing.

        pushed   **pools**

_____

_____
- -

5. I _____ Sam giggle.

        done   **heard**

 **School–Home Connection**

Have your child read each completed sentence
aloud. Then have your child think of a
sentence with the word *pools*.

 19

▶ **Read the story. Then circle the answer for each question.**

Bert Butterfly woke up. "I am going to see my friends," he said. He packed a snack.

He flew up into the sky. "Oh, no!" Bert cried. "I forgot my map! How will I find my way?"

Bert had to think and think. "I will look for the bright red flowers. My friends live close to them."

At last, Bert found his friends. They were happy!

I. Where did this story happen?

2. Who is this story about?

3. What happened at the end?

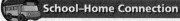 **School–Home Connection**

Read the story with your child. Talk about what happens in the beginning, middle, and ending of the story.

Extra Support
© Harcourt • Grade 1 • Book 5

▶ **Write the word from the box that matches the clue.**

ground	frown	sound
crown	round	

1.  A king has one.

2.  You can stand on this.

3.  You do this when you are sad.

4.  This is the shape of a ball.

Extra Support
© Harcourt • Grade 1 • Book 5

▶ **Write the word from the box that
names the picture.**

candy	field	kitties
party	pennies	snowy

1. party

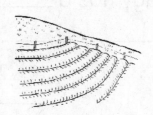

2. _____

3. _____

4. _____

5. _____

6. _____

 School–Home Connection

Have your child read each word aloud.
Together, think of other words that end with
y or *ie*.

 23

Extra Support
© Harcourt • Grade 1 • Book 5

▶ **Circle the word that completes the sentence. Then write the word.**

bun (bunny)

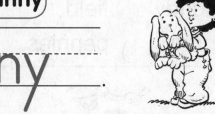

1. Peggy has a __bunny__.

flip floppy

2. Its ears are _____.

field fed

3. They play in a _____.

sleepy slippery

4. Peggy gets _____.

home hungry

5. The bunny gets _____.

25

Extra Support
© Harcourt • Grade 1 • Book 5

▶ **Choose a word to complete the
sentence.**

_____

- -

1. Kelly _____ a long trip.

blue   took

_____

- -

2. She _____ to the seashore.

traveled   able

_____

- -

3. Kelly saw a lot of _____ water.

took   blue

_____

- -

4. She _____ sand into a pail.

poured   almost

_____

- -

5. Kelly was _____ to find seashells.

great   able

 School–Home Connection

Take turns reading each completed sentence
aloud. Encourage your child to use the words
under the lines to make other sentences.

26

► **Read the story. Circle the word that completes the sentence. Then write the word.**

Jim likes to make things with blocks. He makes a small house. It has red blocks for the walls. There are black blocks for the windows. The door is made from blue blocks. Jim uses brown blocks to make a little bed. Jim can make a new block house each day.

(red)   **yellow**

1. The house has _____ **red** _____ blocks for walls.

_____

big   black
_____
- -
2. The windows are _____.

_____

flag   door
_____
- -
3. The house has a blue _____.

School–Home Connection
Read the paragraph with your child. Then
have your child read a sentence that does not
describe Jim's block house.

Extra Support
© Harcourt • Grade 1 • Book 5

Name _____

Phonics: Inflections
-ed, -er, -est, -es
(change *y* to *i*)
Lesson 28

▶ **Write the word that completes the sentence.**

1. He's __worried__ about the sick puppy.

   worry   worried

2. He _____ the trash.

   emptied   emptying

3. Ann tells the _____ jokes in the class.

   funny   funniest

4. Ann is _____ than Mike.

   happier   happy

5. Sam _____ home.

   hurry   hurries

 **School–Home Connection**

Have your child read aloud one of the
sentences he or she completed. Ask how the
two words under the lines are different.

 28

Extra Support
© Harcourt • Grade 1 • Book 5

Name _____

▶ **Write the word from the box that names the picture.**

| boots   grew   moon   moose   noodles |
| room   roof   roots   spoon |

1.

_____

2.

_____

3.

_____

4.

_____

5.

_____

6.

_____

7.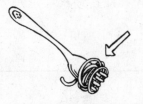

_____

8.

_____

9.

_____

School–Home Connection

Have your child read each word and point to the letters that make the vowel sound heard in *moo*.

30

▶ **Write the word from the box that completes the sentence.**

drew	room	Soon	goose	balloon

I. The _____ is white.

2. I have a red _____ .

3. I _____ a rainbow.

4. Lily plays in her _____ .

5. _____ they will get on the bus.

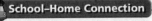

School–Home Connection

Have your child read each completed sentence aloud. Talk about how the words in the box are alike and how they are different.

 32

▶ **Write a word to complete the sentence.**

boy   building

_____

1. This _____ has a train set.

tomorrow   building

_____

2. He is _____ a little city.

boy   toward

_____

3. The train will go _____ the bridge.

welcoming   toward

_____

4. The boy has a _____ smile.

toward   tomorrow

_____

5. The boy will play more _____.

School–Home Connection

Have your child read each sentence with the
correct word from the box. Then ask your
child to write new sentences using some of
these words.

33

▶ **Read the story. Then answer the questions.**

It is a sunny day. Mom and Nancy are going on a picnic. They put ice in a cooler. Nancy puts a ham sandwich in the cooler. Mom puts in an egg sandwich. Mom chooses grapes and peaches for a snack. Nancy adds some water bottles. Now they can go!

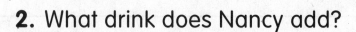

1. Who will go on a picnic?

○ Jack
○ Dad and Nancy
○ Mom and Nancy

_____

2. What drink does Nancy add?

○ water
○ milk
○ ice

_____

3. What snack does Mom choose?

○ apples
○ grapes and peaches
○ chips

 School–Home Connection

Read the story aloud with your child. Ask him or her to name something other than food and water that was packed in the cooler. *(ice)*

Extra Support
© Harcourt • Grade 1 • Book 5

Name _____

▶ **Read the chart. Then write the contraction that completes the sentence.**

They	have	They've
can	not	can't
She	is	She's
He	would	He'd
I	will	I'll

1. _____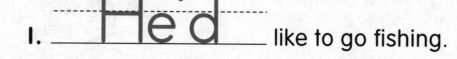_____ like to go fishing.

2. _____ starting a campfire.

3. They _____ play in the rain.

4. _____ been hoping it will stop.

5. I am sleepy. _____ take a nap.

School–Home Connection

Have your child read aloud one of the
sentences he or she completed. Ask how
the words in the chart changed from one
column to the other.

35

▶ **Write the word from the box that
names the picture.**

robot	ivy	child	hippo	tiger	yo-yo

1. child

2. _____

3. _____

4. _____

5. _____

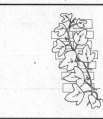

6. _____

Extra Support
© Harcourt • Grade 1 • Book 5

▶ **Write the word from the box that completes the sentence.**

go	won't	cold	find	Friday

_____
- - - - - - - - - - - - - - - - - -

1. Jenny can't _____ her coat.

_____
- - - - - - - - - - - - - - - - - -

2. She had it last _____ .

_____
- - - - - - - - - - - - - - - - - -

3. She can't _____ out.

_____
- - - - - - - - - - - - - - - - - -

4. She will get _____ .

_____
- - - - - - - - - - - - - - - - - -

5. Jenny _____ stop looking.

School–Home Connection

Have your child read each completed sentence aloud. Together, think of words that rhyme with some of the words in the box.

▶ **Write a word from the box to complete the sentence.**

any	front	nothing
ready	sorry	

_____

1. Owl came to Bird's _____ door.

_____

2. "Are you _____ to go?" he asked.

_____

3. "I'm _____, but I can't go," said Bird.

_____

4. "I don't have _____ hat or scarf."

Try This

Use the word <u>nothing</u> to write a new sentence.

 School–Home Connection

Ask your child to read each completed sentence. Point to the words *any* and *nothing*. Take turns using the words in sentences.

40

Name _____

► **Fill in the circle in front of the word
that comes first in ABC order.**

1. ● airport   ○ store   ○ jail

_____

2. ○ yard   ○ park   ○ haystack

_____

3. ○ mill   ○ zoo   ○ tower

_____

4. ○ field   ○ backyard   ○ campsite

_____

5. ○ classroom   ○ firehouse   ○ bakery

_____

6. ○ jungle   ○ farm   ○ pool

_____

7. ○ beach   ○ shipyard   ○ cave

_____

8. ○ school   ○ mall   ○ circus

Extra Support
© Harcourt • Grade 1 • Book 5

Name _____

► **Write the word from the box that names the picture.**

old	hold	cold	gold	fold	sold

1. **gold**

2. _____

3. _____

4. _____

5. _____

6. _____

School–Home Connection

Have your child read each word aloud. Talk about how the words are the same and how they are different.

42

Answer Key

Book 1

Page 2
1. a
2. a
3. Leave blank.
4. a
5. a
6. a
7. Leave blank.
8. a
9. Leave blank.

Page 4
1. bag
2. cap
3. bat
4. nap
5. can
6. man
7. mat
8. pan
9. jam

Page 5
1. help
2. now
3. Let's

Page 6
1. bat
2. ran
3. nap

Page 7
1. hats
2. maps
3. bags
4. vans
5. wags
6. taps

Page 9
1. cat
2. van
3. map
4. ham
5. fan
6. tag

7. bat
8. hat
9. ran

Page 11
1. map
2. cap
3. naps
4. bat
5. cat

Page 12
1. in
2. too
3. no

Page 13
1. Jan had a nap.
2. Max has ham.
3. The cat ran.

Page 14
1. band
2. rag
3. hand
4. sand
5. bag

Page 16
1. i
2. i
3. i
4. Leave blank.
5. i
6. Leave blank.
7. i
8. i
9. Leave blank.

Page 18
1. six
2. mitt
3. pin
4. hit
5. wig
6. lip
7. fist
8. lid
9. dig

Page 19
1. Get
2. so
3. Hold
4. soon
5. home

Page 20
1. pictures of a wool cap and a top hat
2. pictures of a chair and a bed
3. pictures of a banana and a watermelon
4. pictures of a crayon and a marker

Page 21
1. it's
2. here's
3. he's
4. she's
5. where's
6. what's
7. there's
8. that's

Page 23
1. tack
2. back
3. lick
4. sick
5. kick
6. sack

Page 25
1. tack
2. back
3. lick
4. sick
5. kick
6. sack

Page 26
1. late
2. Oh
3. Yes

A1

Page 27

1, 3, 2
Accept reasonable responses.

Page 28
1. fill
2. sit
3. will
4. it
5. hill

Page 30
1. o
2. o
3. o
4. Leave blank.
5. Leave blank.
6. o
7. Leave blank.
8. o

Page 32
1. mop
2. pot
3. fox
4. lock
5. sock
6. log
7. rock
8. doll
9. box

Page 33
1. thank
2. much
3. find
4. much
5. thank

Page 34
1. Cat
2. Dog
3. Jill

Page 35
1. camping
2. thanked
3. kicked
4. looking

Page 37
1. tall

2. ball
3. fall
4. call
5. wall
6. hall

Page 39
1. call
2. tall
3. ball
4. mall
5. all
6. hall

Page 40
1. some
2. make
3. of
4. How

Page 41
1. Circle the two socks.
2. Circle the two balls.
3. Circle the truck and the van.
4. Circle the cat and the fish.

Page 42
1. isn't
2. can't
3. aren't
4. didn't
5. he's
6. she's
7. that's
8. who's

Book 2

Page 2
1. bed
2. pet
3. nest
4. hen
5. web
6. ten
7. jet
8. leg
9. net

Page 4
1. e
2. e
3. e
4. e
5. Leave blank.
6. Leave blank.
7. e
8. Leave blank.
9. e

Page 5
1. was
2. said
3. first
4. eat
5. time

Page 6
Accept reasonable responses.

Page 7
1. fl
2. fl
3. bl
4. cl
5. pl

Page 9
1. th
2. Leave blank.
3. th
4. Leave blank.
5. Leave blank.
6. th
7. Leave blank.
8. th
9. Leave blank.

Page 11
1. math
2. bath
3. This
4. thin
5. That

Page 12
1. says
2. water
3. her
4. don't
5. new

Page 13
1. dog
2. jump
3. fat
4. soft

Page 14
1. sw
2. sk
3. st
4. sp
5. sl

Page 16
1. bug
2. cup
3. hug
4. nut
5. bus
6. run

Page 18
1. u
2. u
3. Leave blank.
4. u
5. u
6. Leave blank.
7. u
8. u
9. Leave blank.

Page 19
1. live
2. grow
3. does
4. Many
5. food

Page 20
1. a pot
2. tall
3. Two buds
4. pink

Page 21
1. cr
2. dr
3. dr
4. gr
5. tr

Page 23
1. ng
2. ng
3. Leave blank.
4. ng
5. ng
6. ng
7. Leave blank.
8. Leave blank.
9. ng

Page 25
1. hang
2. long
3. stung
4. swung
5. bangs

Page 26
1. school
2. your
3. way
4. arms
5. feet
6. every

Page 27
1. Stan wants to swim.
2. Dad has a lot to do.
3. Mom and Stan help Dad.
4. They all go to swim.

Page 28
1. I'll
2. They'll
3. He'll
4. It'll

Page 30
1. stork
2. corn
3. forest
4. cord
5. fork
6. horn
7. thorn
8. storm
9. sport

Page 32
1. Corn
2. fork
3. morning
4. thorns
5. forest

Page 33
1. fish
2. under
3. cold
4. animals
5. very

Page 34
First group: circle shoes, meal, bedroom; second group: circle dish, bed, collar.

Page 35
1. bathtub
2. sunset
3. popcorn
4. kickball
5. anthill
6. backpack

Page 37
1. fish
2. ship
3. dish
4. shell
5. cash
6. shed

Page 39
1. wish
2. mash
3. shack
4. short
5. cash
6. shop

Page 40
1. gold
2. happy
3. came
4. could
5. made

A3

Page 41

1. Draw a line to picture of school and bus.
2. Draw a line to picture of the beach.
3. Draw a line to picture of barn and pig.

Page 42

1. cl
2. sw
3. fl
4. st
5. dr

Book 3

Page 2

1. Trace "ch."
2. Trace "ch."
3. Cross out "ch."
4. Trace "ch."
5. Trace "ch."
6. Trace "ch."
7. Trace "ch."
8. Trace "ch."
9. Cross out "ch."

Page 4

1. watch
2. catch
3. patch
4. lunch
5. chin
6. chest

Page 5

1. fly
2. air
3. friends
4. watch
5. need

Page 6

1, 3, 2
Accept reasonable responses.

Page 7

1. fixes
2. matches
3. tosses
4. brushes
5. dishes

Page 9

1. barn
2. farm
3. shark
4. scarf
5. yarn
6. arm
7. car
8. march
9. cart

Page 11

1. card
2. stars
3. far
4. park
5. barn

Page 12

1. house
2. Mrs.
3. know
4. say
5. put

Page 13

1. Liz Smith wants us to know how to help lost pets.
2. picture of Liz Smith

Page 14

1. fishing
2. checked
3. grilled
4. helps
5. itching

Page 16

1. quilt
2. quit
3. When
4. quick
5. quacks

Page 18

1. qu
2. Wh
3. qu
4. Qu
5. wh

Page 19

1. books
2. writing
3. read
4. about
5. name
6. work

Page 20

3, 1, 2
1. First, a hen sits on her egg.
2. Next, the egg hatches.
3. Last, a chick comes out of the egg.

Page 21

1. stopped
2. stopping
3. clipped
4. clipping
5. mopped
6. mopping

Page 23

1. bird
2. curl
3. girl
4. skirt
5. first
6. dirt
7. stir
8. third
9. burn

Page 25

1. shirt
2. turnip
3. hurt
4. fur
5. curb
6. fern

Page 26
1. join
2. room
3. Please
4. always
5. nice

Page 27
1. The birds have a bath.
2. The ostrich came in first.
3. Rabbit went to the market.
4. Jack has a good book.
5. There's a skunk in my yard!
6. Dan forgot his lunch.

Page 28
1. smallest
2. faster
3. softer
4. smartest

Page 30
1. bottle
2. turtle
3. candle
4. kettle
5. rattle
6. apple
7. fiddle
8. puddle
9. buckle

Page 32
1. bubble
2. turtle
3. pickle
4. ankle
5. paddle
6. juggle

Page 33
1. money
2. buy
3. paper
4. carry
5. paint

Page 34
1. Many animals live in ponds.

Page 35
1. hopped–hopping
2. napped–napping
3. mopped–mopping
4. hopping
5. mopped

Page 37
1. bow
2. goat
3. boat
4. toast
5. mow
6. soap
7. coat
8. road

Page 39
1. coat
2. road
3. snow
4. crow
5. bowl
6. toad

Page 40
1. our
2. over
3. three
4. surprise
5. mouse

Page 41
1. Brent Hall wants us to know what plants need to grow.

Page 42
1. grown
2. roast
3. thrown
4. own
5. coast

Book 4

Page 2
1. beans
2. eagle
3. three
4. team
5. feet

6. she
7. jeep
8. leaf
9. needle

Page 4
1. tree
2. jeans
3. leak
4. eat
5. peach
6. queen
7. seed
8. sheep

Page 5
1. mother
2. door
3. hurry
4. sky
5. should

Page 6
1. She dropped the cup.
2. He is sick.
3. The sun melted the snow.
4. They like the play.

Page 7
1. I've
2. They're
3. We've
4. You're
5. We're

Page 9
1. hay
2. stain
3. rain
4. paint
5. play
6. tray
7. train
8. chain
9. pay

Page 11
1. nails
2. day
3. play
4. rain
5. braids

Page 12
1. warm
2. dry
3. cool
4. place
5. holes

Page 13
1. It is raining.
2. The wind is blowing hard.
3. It is cold outside.
4. The sun is very bright.

Page 14
1. snail
2. sail
3. mail
4. pail
5. laid

Page 16
1. a
2. a
3. Leave blank.
4. a
5. a
6. Leave blank.
7. a
8. a
9. Leave blank.

Page 18
1. cape
2. plane
3. lake
4. rake
5. skate
6. snake
7. tape
8. plate
9. whale

Page 19
1. hears
2. around
3. near
4. open
5. found

Page 20
1. picture of a girl pumping up a flat tire
2. picture of a boy closing a window
3. picture of a girl leashing a dog
4. picture of a family mending a fence

Page 21
1. cane
2. made
3. plane
4. Jane
5. Shane

Page 23
1. bike
2. slide
3. pine
4. nine
5. fire
6. hive
7. kite
8. dime
9. tire

Page 25
1. dime
2. ride
3. bite
4. kite
5. shine

Page 26
1. walked
2. right
3. Those
4. light
5. because

Page 27
1. He could get a backpack.
2. She could put on a raincoat.
3. He could take a nap.

Page 28
1. tired
2. smiling

Page 30
3. waved
4. skating

Page 30
1. globe
2. nose
3. home
4. stove
5. rose
6. smoke
7. rope
8. hose
9. note

Page 32
1. hope
2. note
3. robe
4. stove
5. Those

Page 33
1. city
2. hello
3. brown
4. loudly
5. love

Page 34
1. Kate has a birthday.
2. Dave likes fish.
3. Rose wants to be a vet.
4. He went to the store.

Page 35
1. one
2. one
3. ole
4. ole
5. one

Page 37
1. bridge
2. ice
3. badge
4. pencil
5. stage
6. circle

Page 39
1. race
2. space

3. cage
4. page

Page 40
1. eyes
2. visitor
3. talk
4. listen
5. remembered

Page 41
1. Jan likes animals.
2. It is a hot day.
3. Ned's cat is lost.
4. It is Meg's birthday.

Page 42
1. Ben's
2. He's
3. He'll
4. didn't
5. can't

Book 5

Page 2
1. u
2. Leave blank.
3. Leave blank.
4. Leave blank.
5. u
6. u
7. Leave blank.
8. u
9. Leave blank.

Page 4
1. huge
2. mule
3. flute
4. tune
5. cube

Page 5
1. kinds
2. hair
3. clear
4. color
5. good-bye

Page 6
1. duck
2. ape

3. bee
4. crow
5. mule
6. rat
7. bird

Page 7
1. waved
2. waving
3. tugged
4. tugging
5. used
6. using

Page 9
1. fly
2. pie
3. light
4. fry
5. tie
6. sky
7. night
8. cry
9. high

Page 11
1. dried
2. might
3. try
4. high

Page 12
1. earth
2. thought
3. climbed
4. fooling
5. table

Page 13
1. picture of a creek
2. picture of a beaver
3. picture of beaver's home

Page 14
1. I'd
2. They're
3. You're
4. We've

Page 16
1. owl
2. house

3. mouth
4. cow
5. cloud
6. flower

Page 18
1. mouse
2. out
3. couch
4. found
5. house

Page 19
1. answered
2. together
3. baby
4. pushed
5. heard

Page 20
1. picture of the sky
2. picture of Bert Butterfly
3. picture of Bert Butterfly and his friends

Page 21
1. crown
2. ground
3. frown
4. round

Page 23
1. party
2. field
3. candy
4. snowy
5. kitties
6. pennies

Page 25
1. bunny
2. floppy
3. field
4. sleepy
5. hungry

Page 26
1. took
2. traveled
3. blue
4. poured
5. able

Extra Support
© Harcourt • Grade 1

Page 27
1. red
2. black
3. door

Page 28
1. worried
2. emptied
3. funniest
4. happier
5. hurries

Page 30
1. boots
2. moon
3. roots
4. spoon
5. grew
6. moose
7. noodles
8. room
9. roof

Page 32
1. goose
2. balloon
3. drew
4. room
5. Soon

Page 33
1. boy
2. building
3. toward
4. welcoming
5. tomorrow

Page 34
1. Mom and Nancy
2. water
3. grapes and peaches

Page 35
1. He'd
2. She's
3. can't
4. They've
5. I'll

Page 37
1. child
2. tiger

3. yo-yo
4. robot
5. hippo
6. ivy

Page 39
1. find
2. Friday
3. go
4. cold
5. won't

Page 40
1. front
2. ready
3. sorry
4. any

Page 41
1. airport
2. haystack
3. mill
4. backyard
5. bakery
6. farm
7. beach
8. circus

Page 42
1. gold
2. fold
3. old
4. cold
5. hold
6. sold

HARCOURT SCHOOL PUBLISHERS

STORYtown

Extra Support

Copying Masters

Grade 1

Harcourt School Publishers